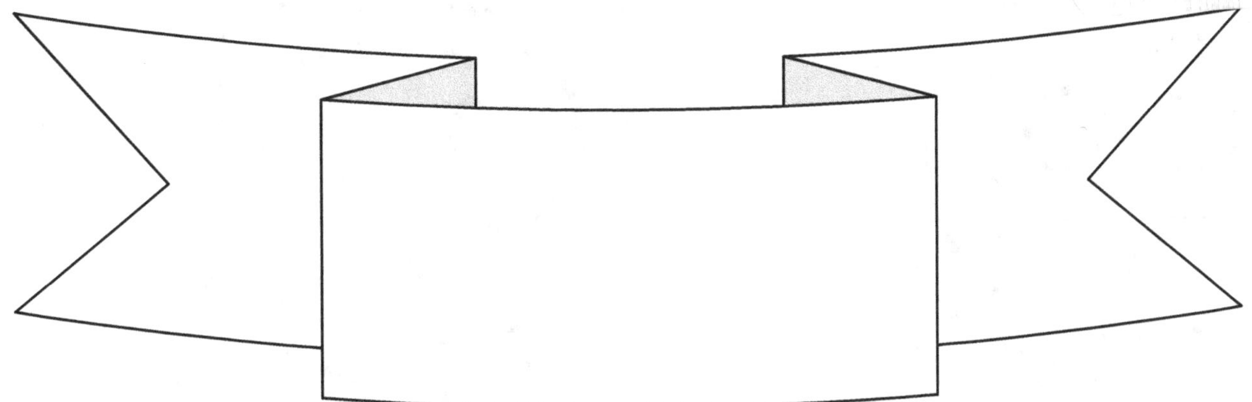

COLORING
BOOK

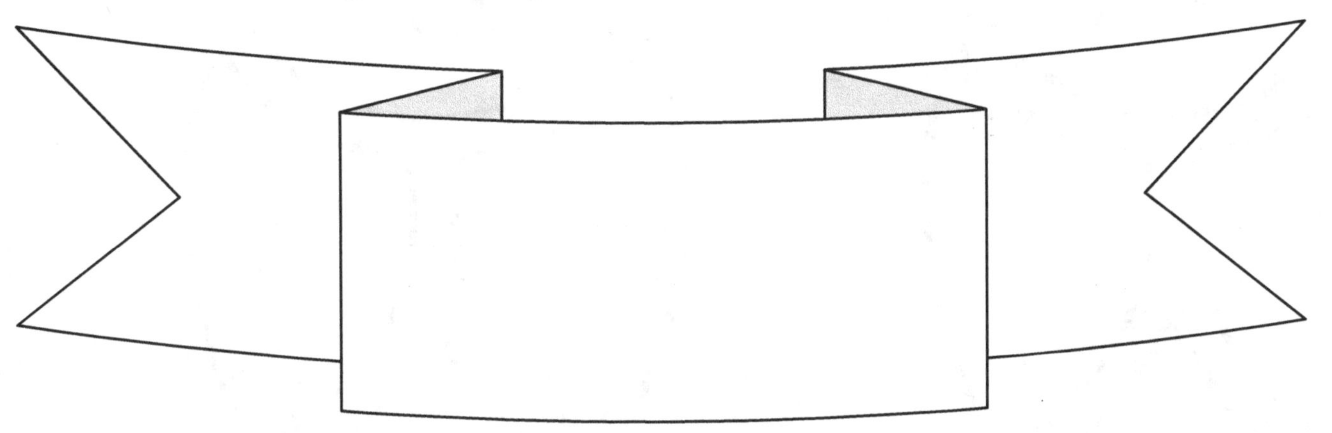

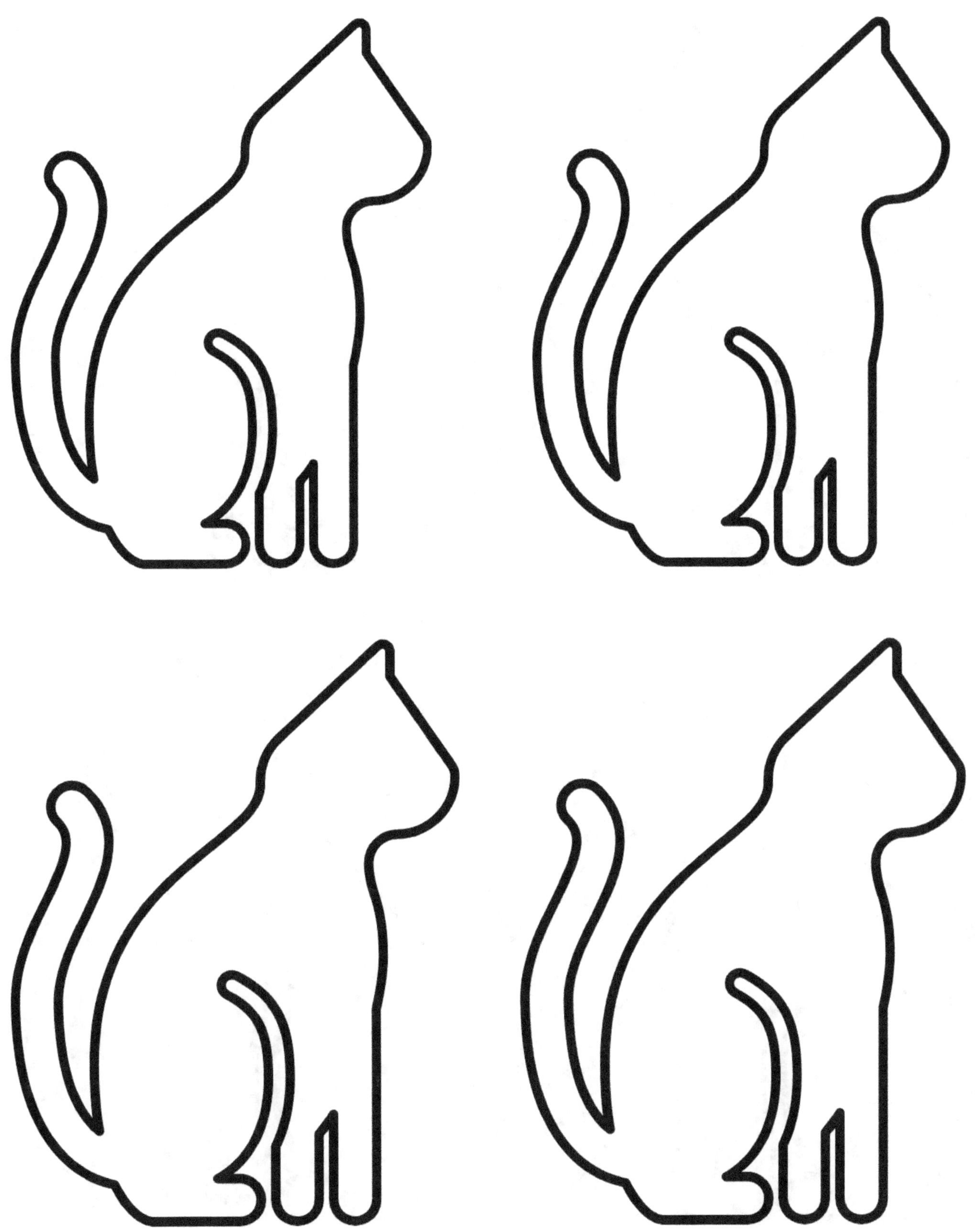

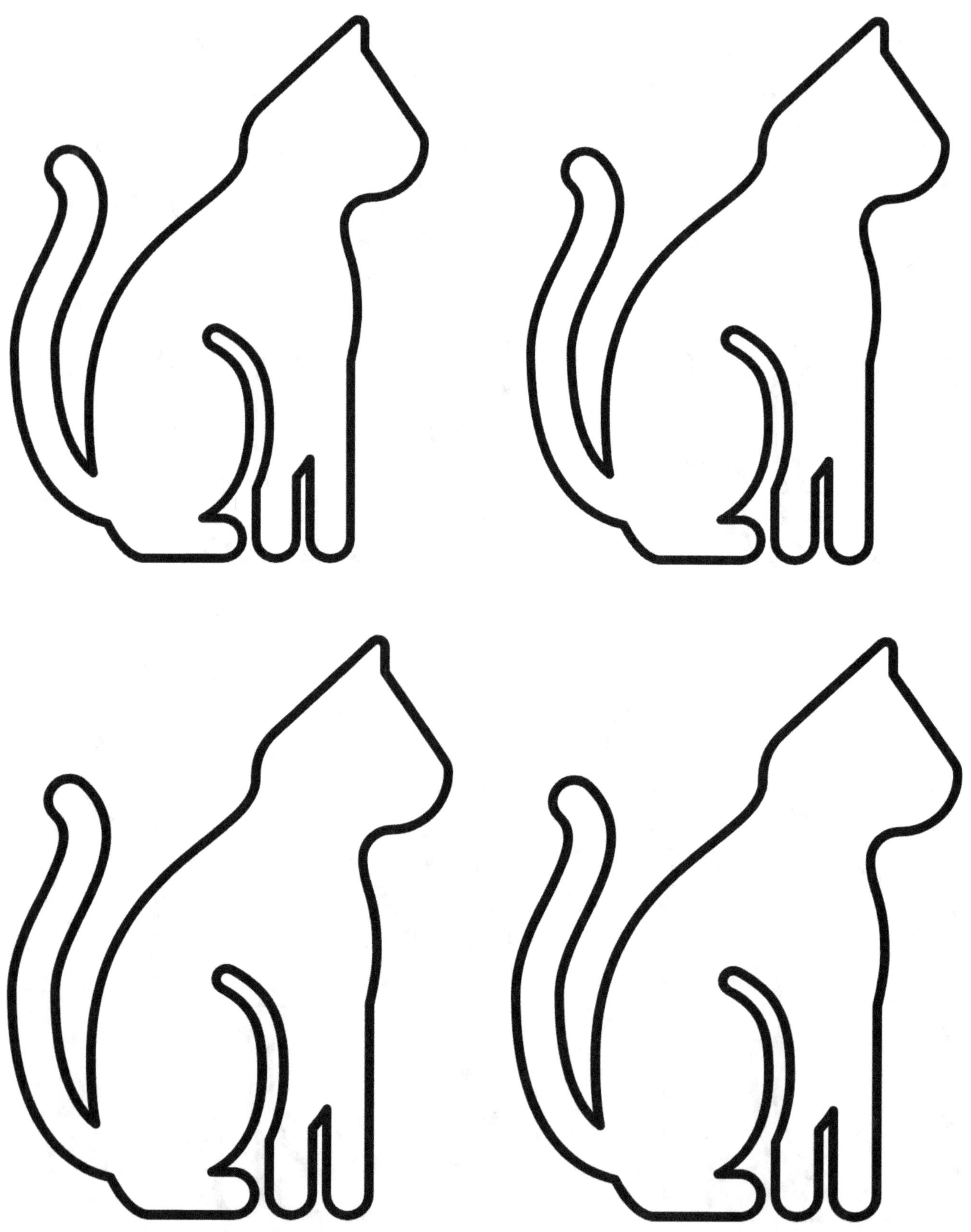

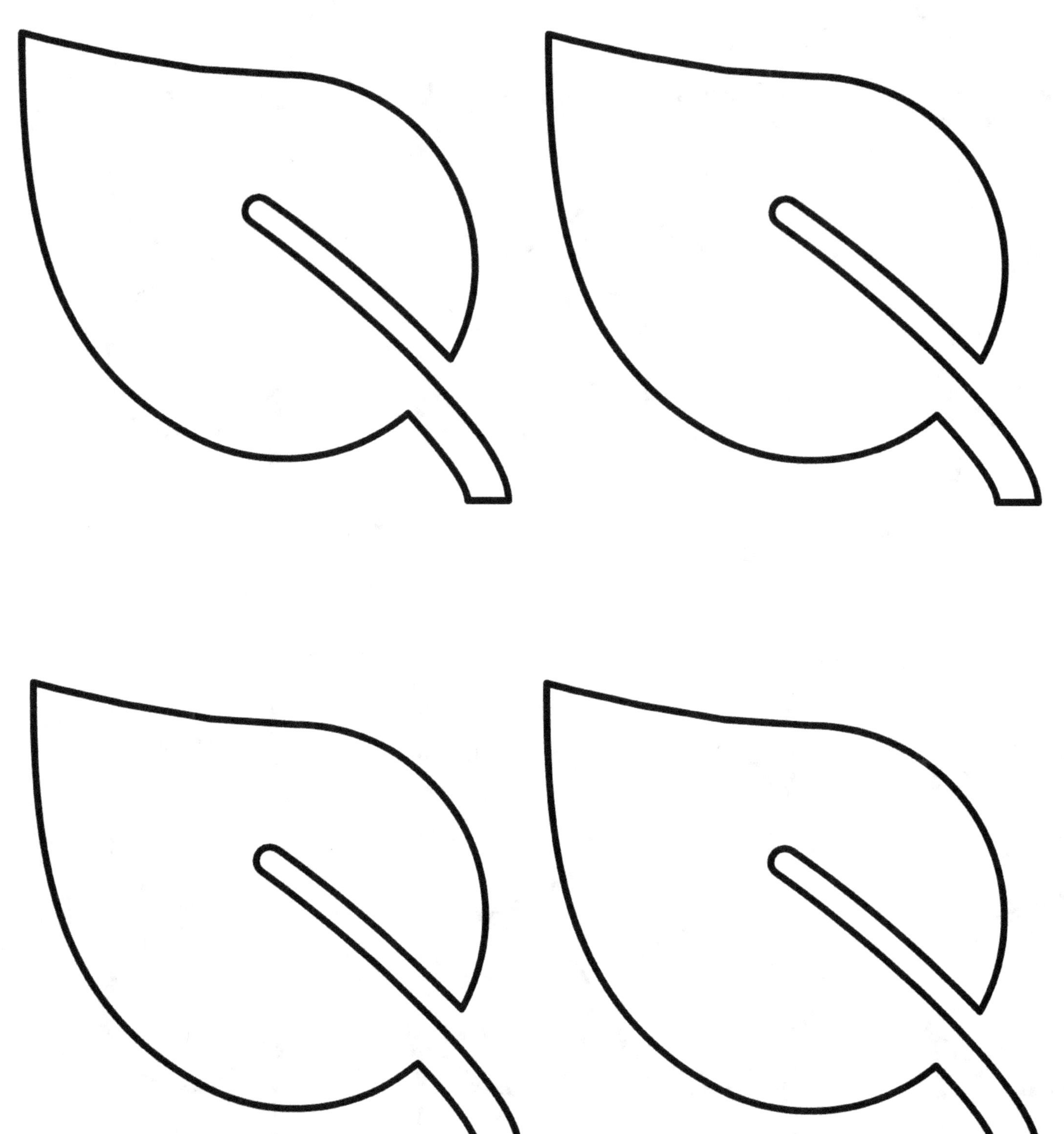

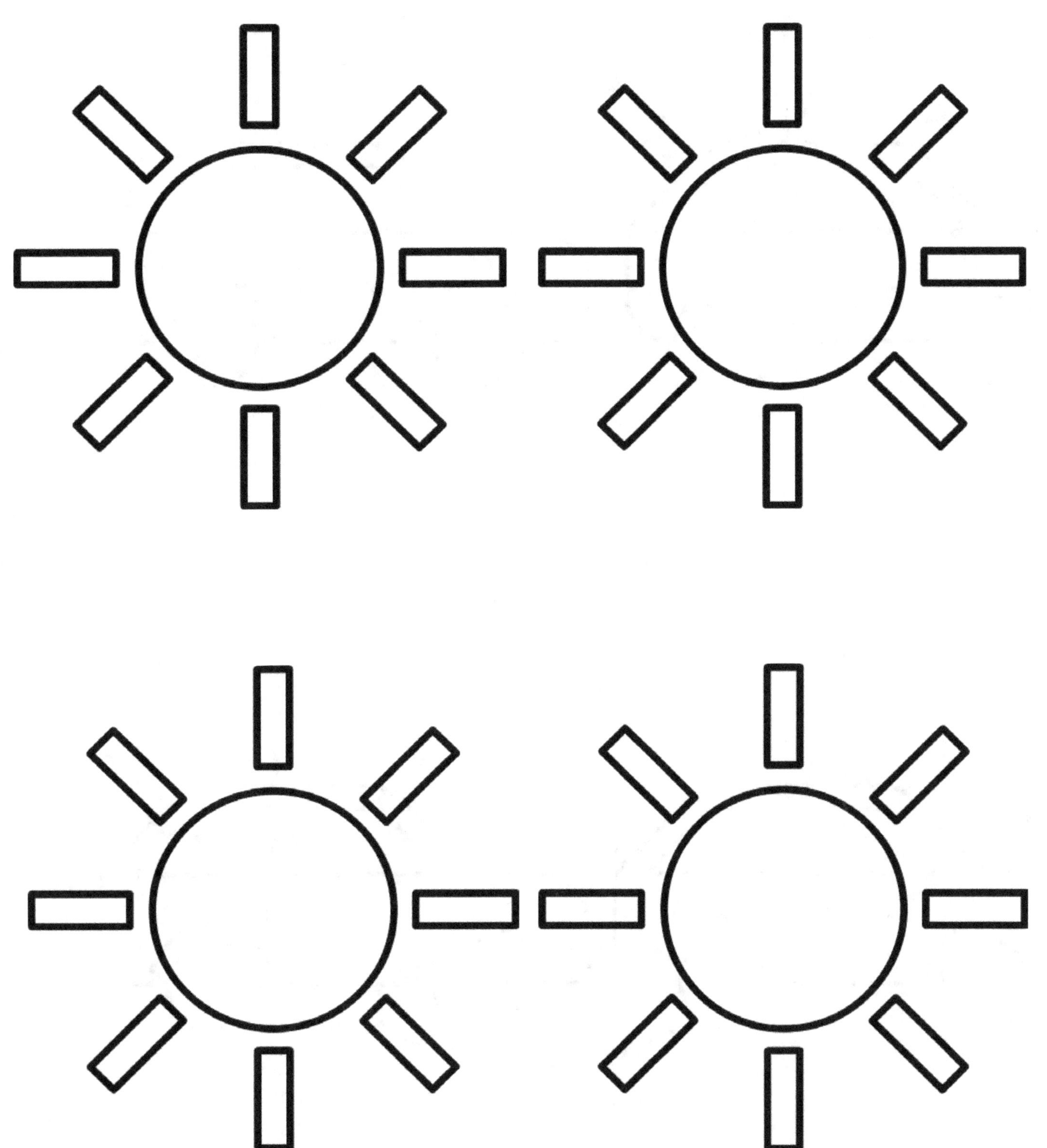

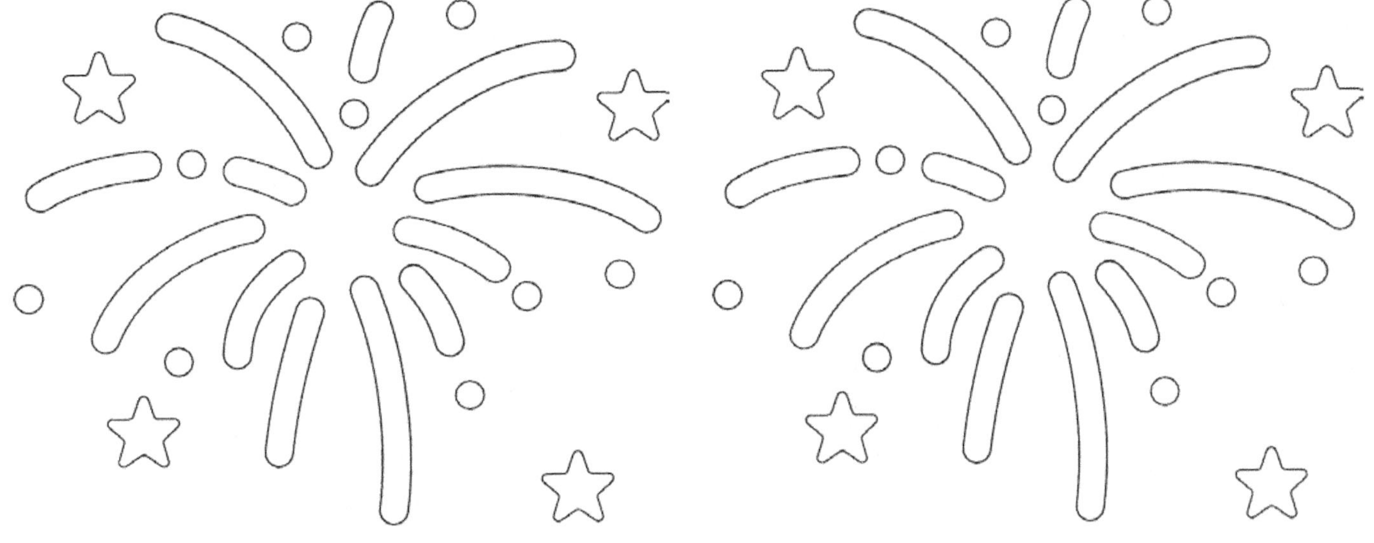

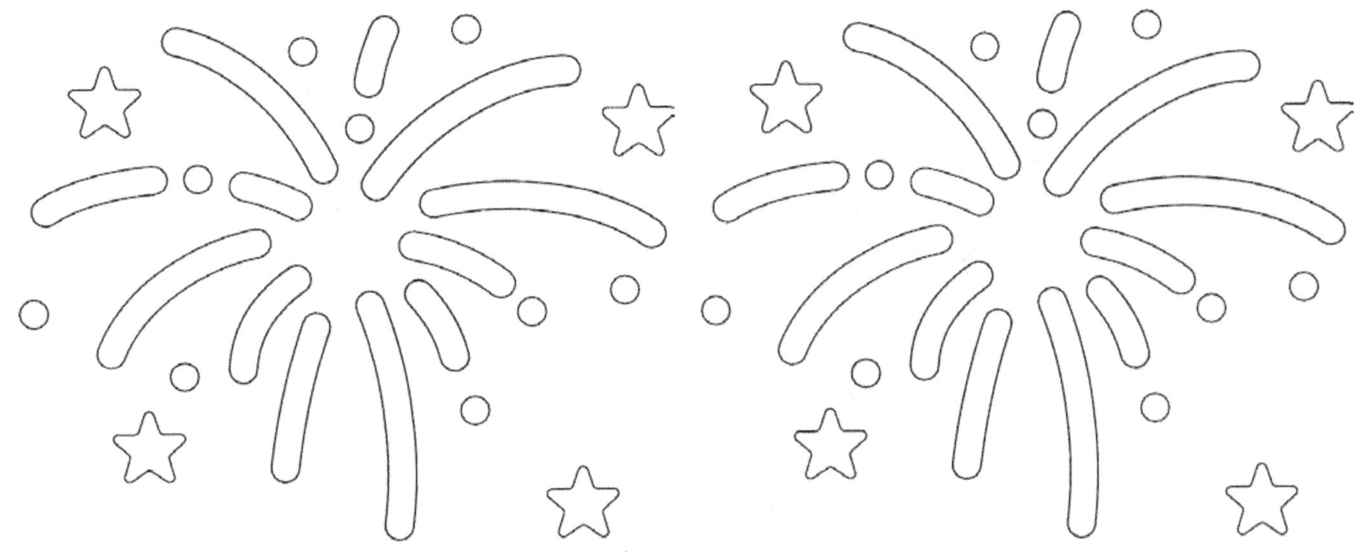

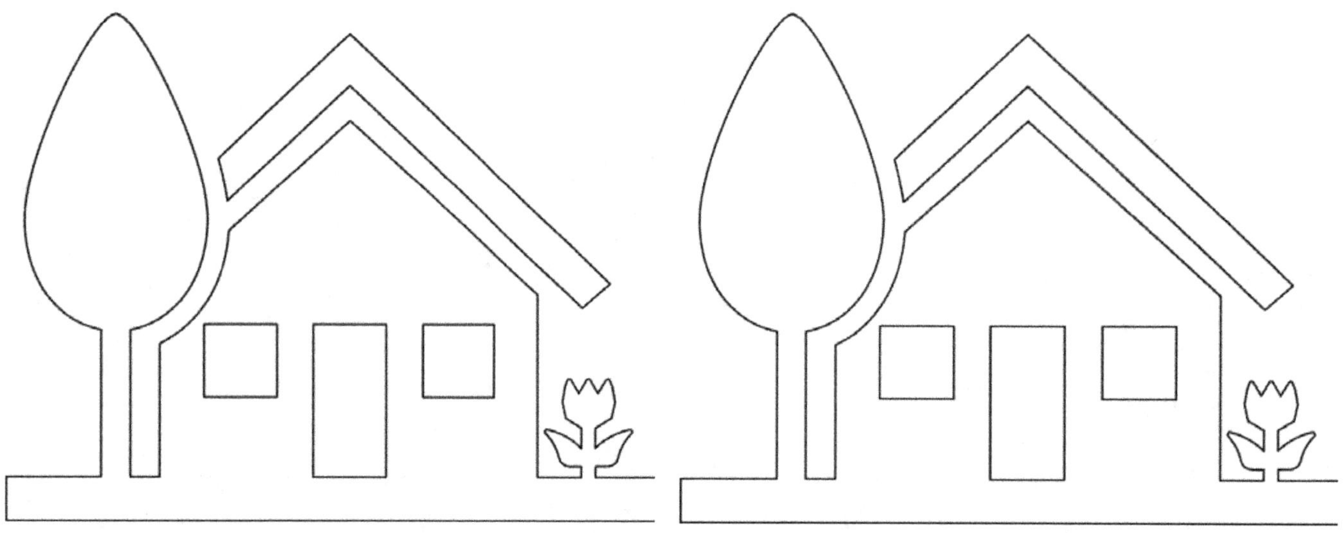

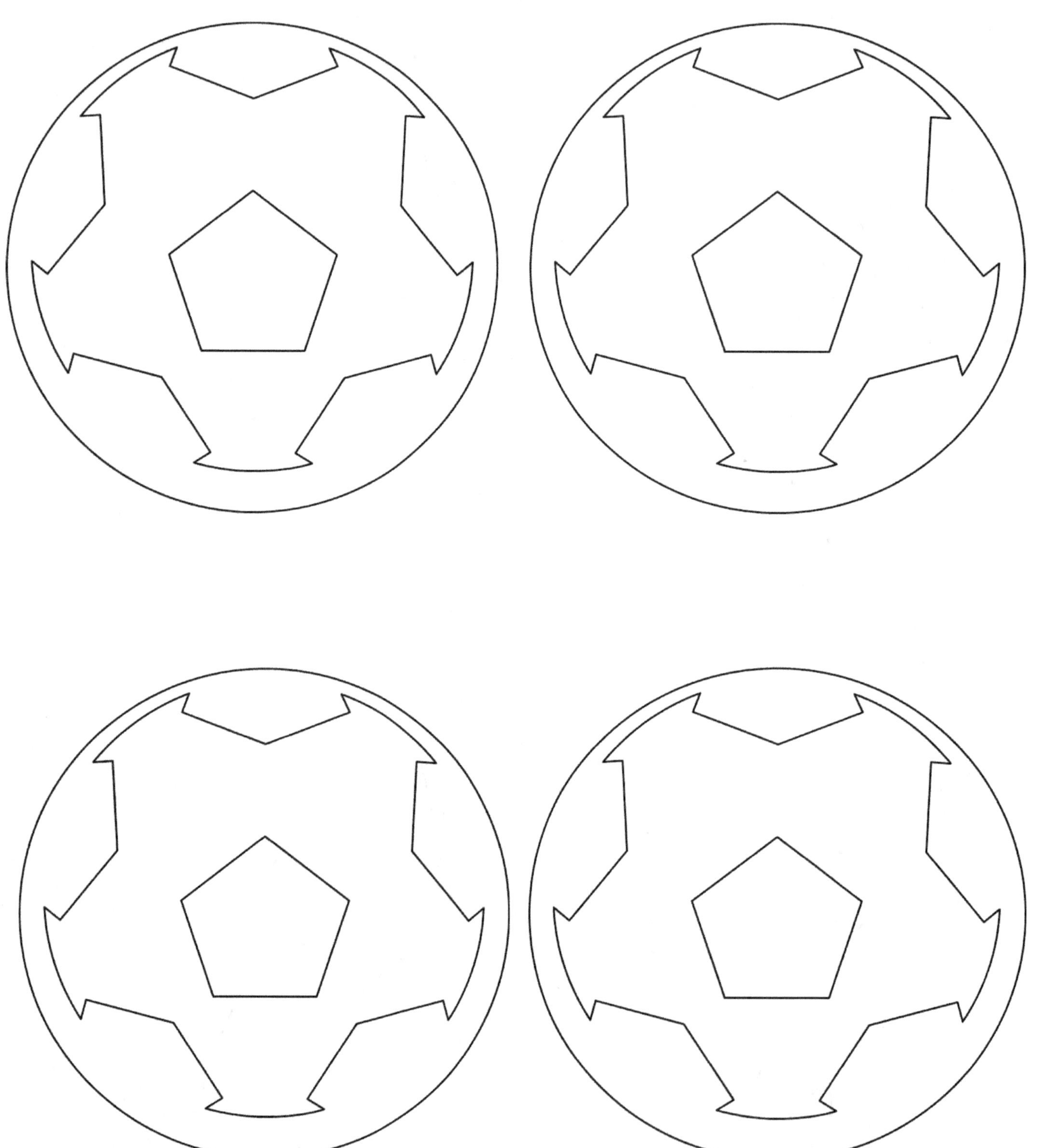

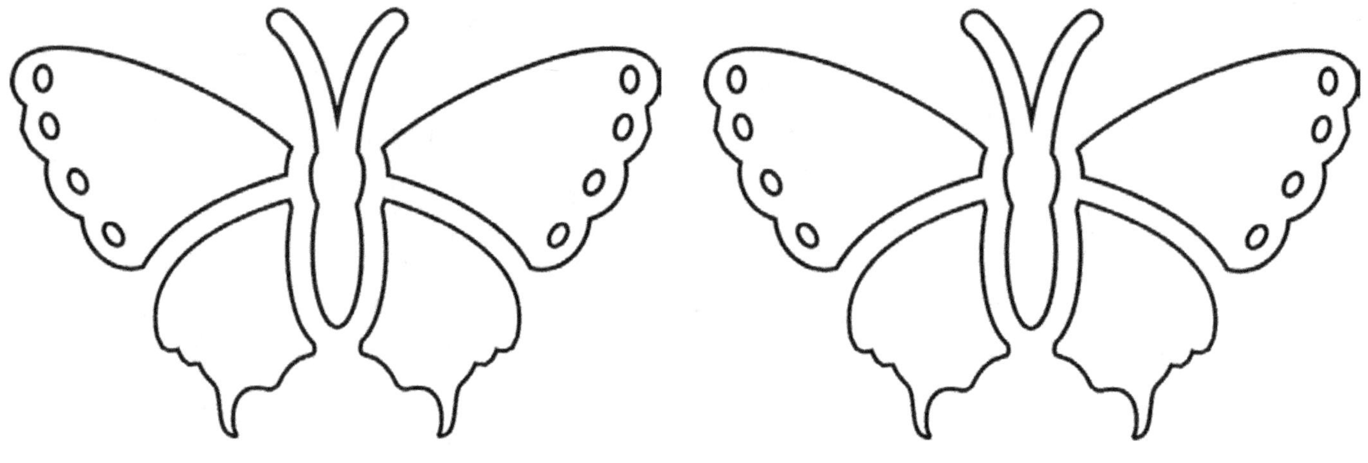

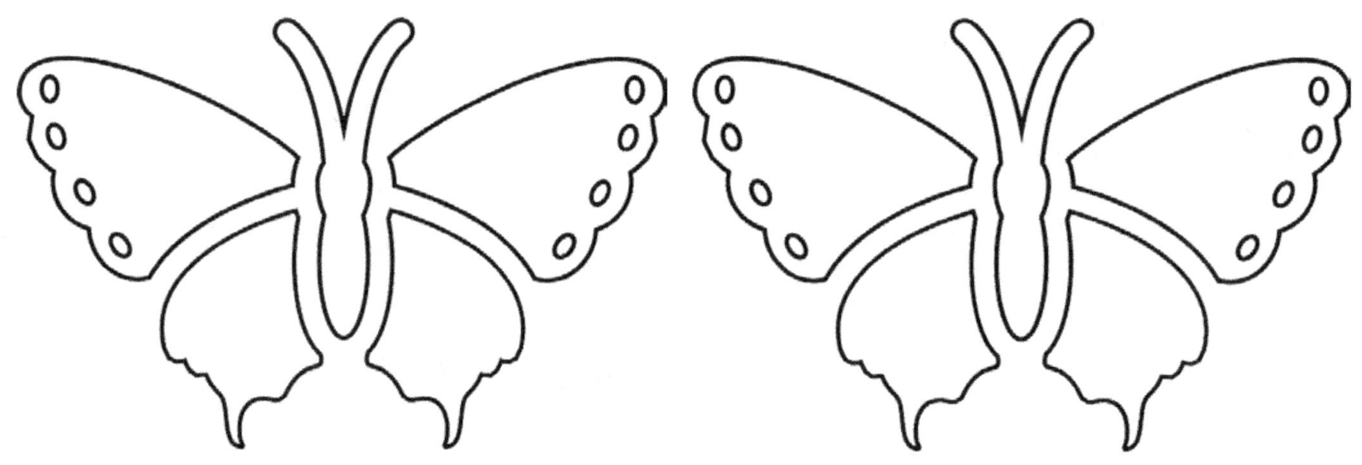

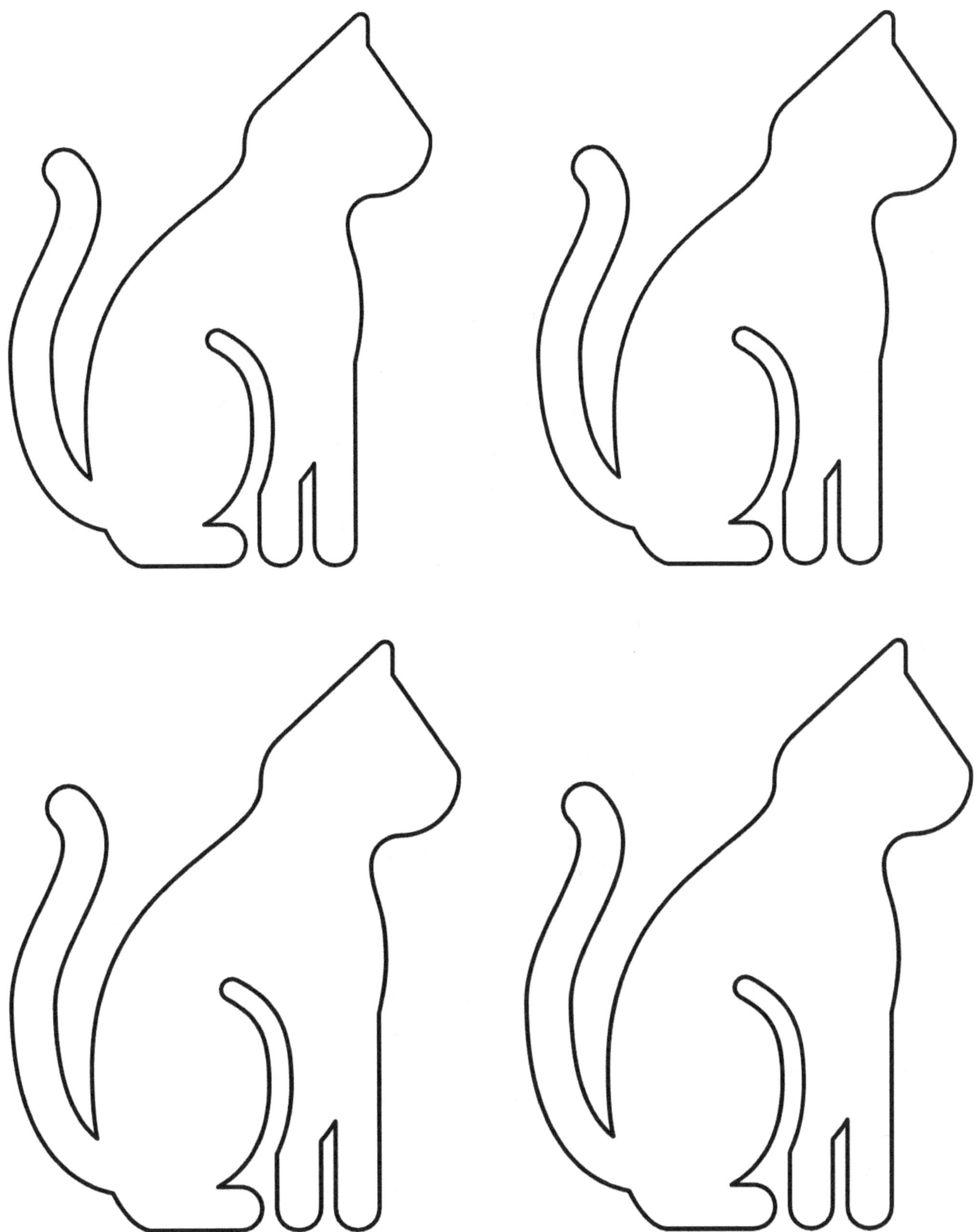

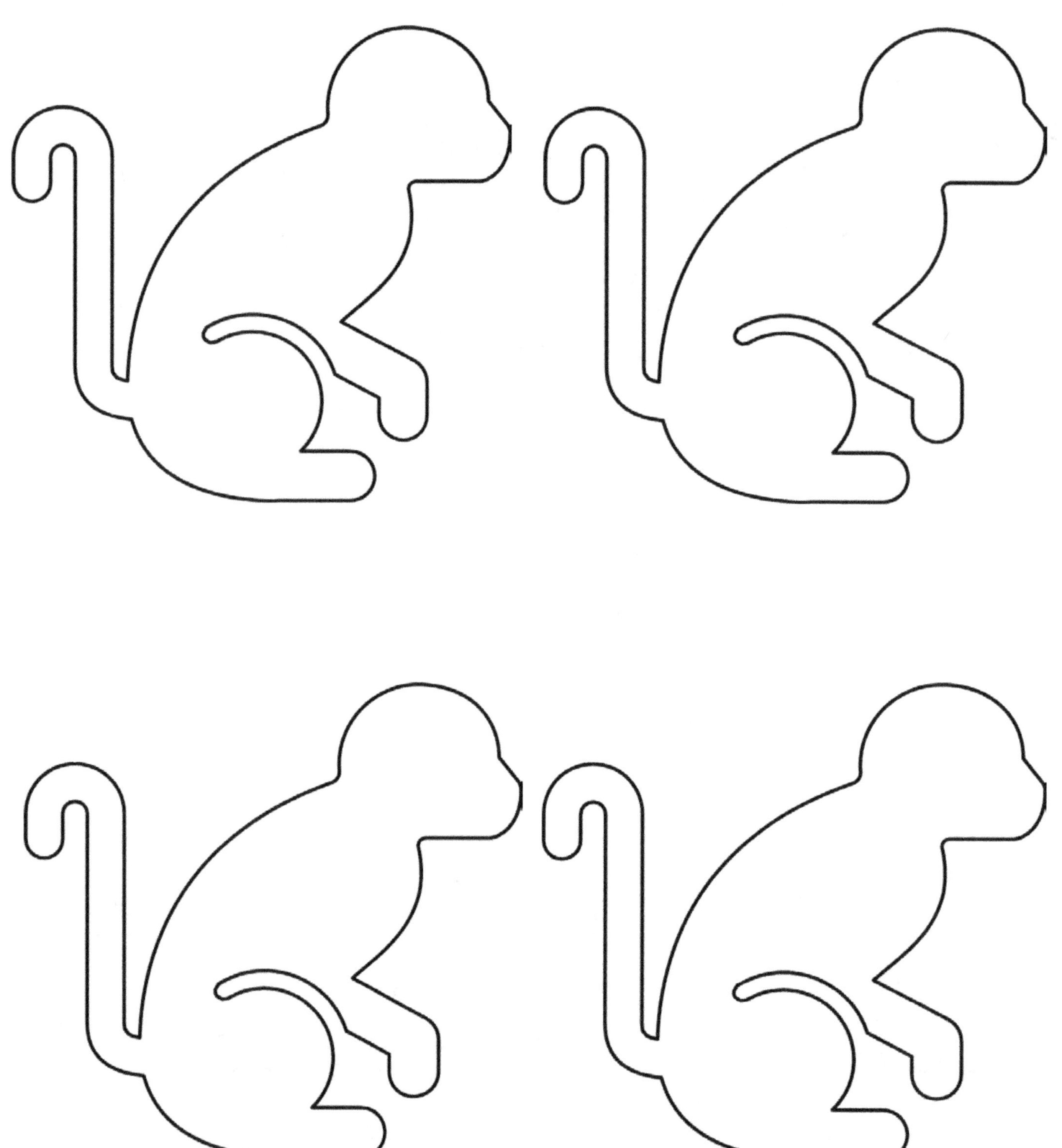

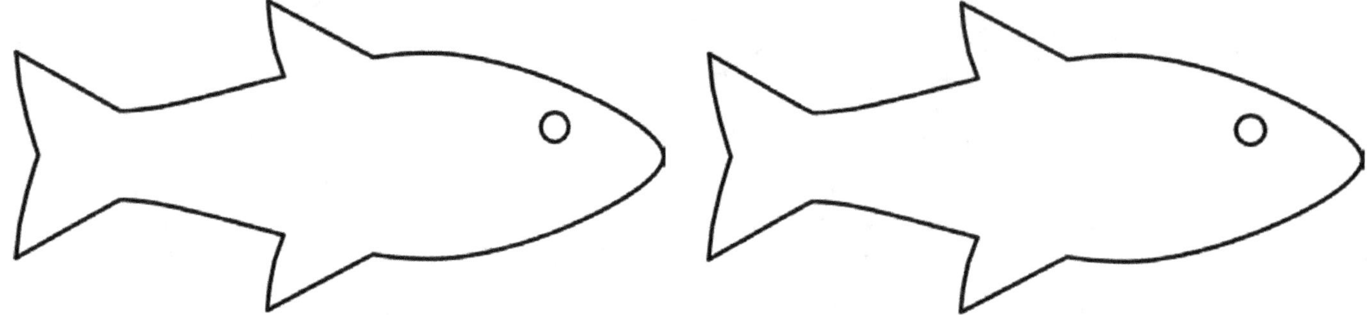
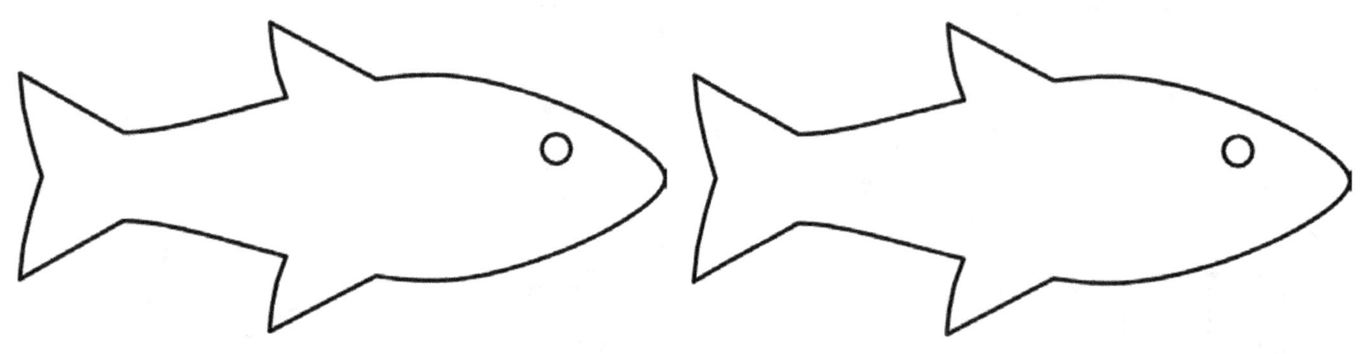

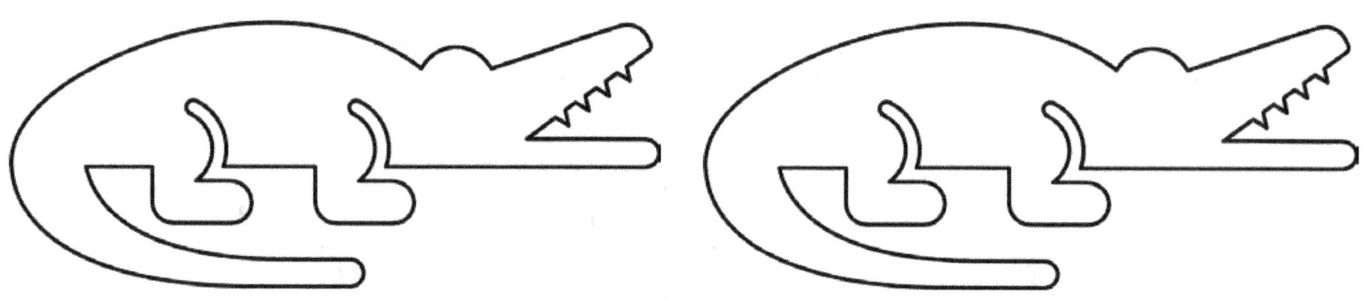
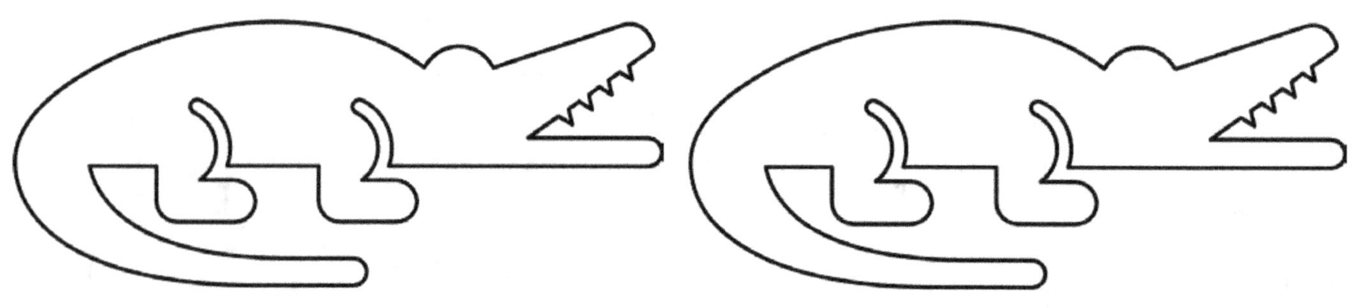

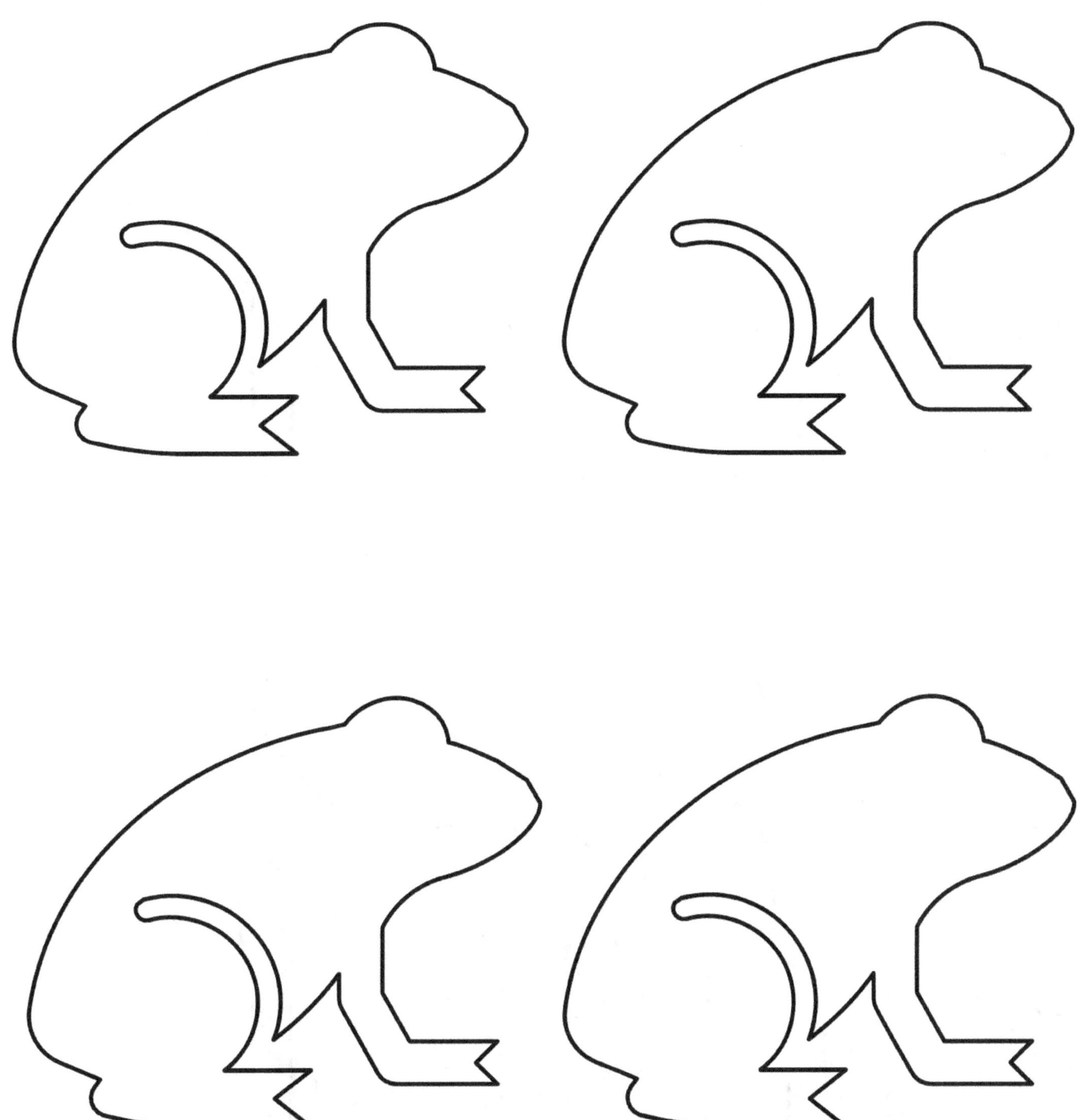

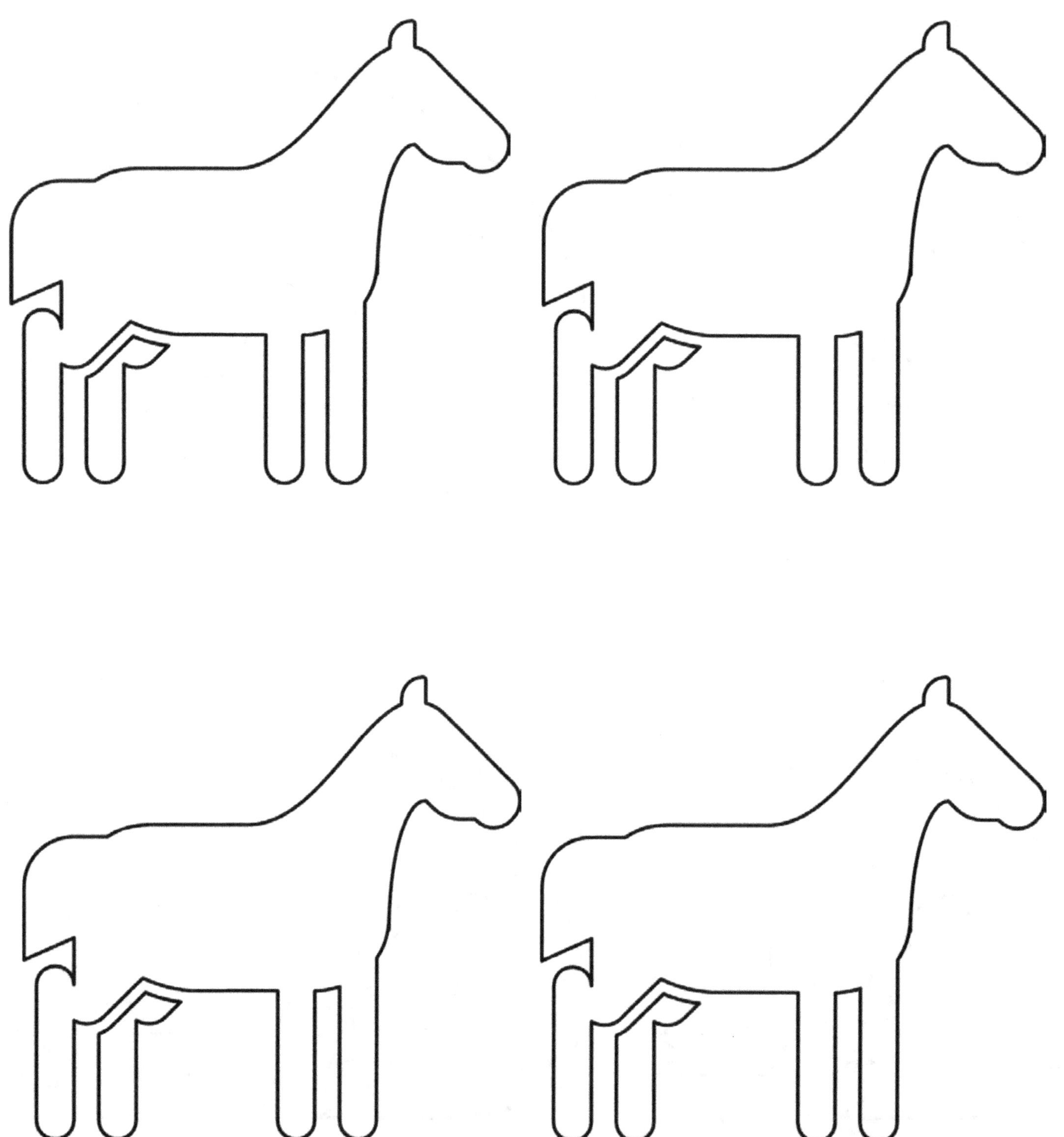

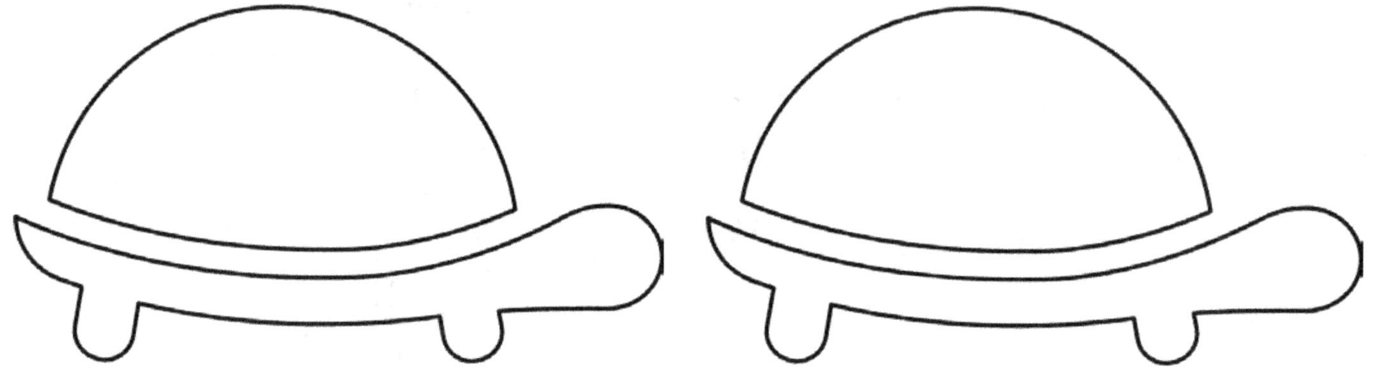

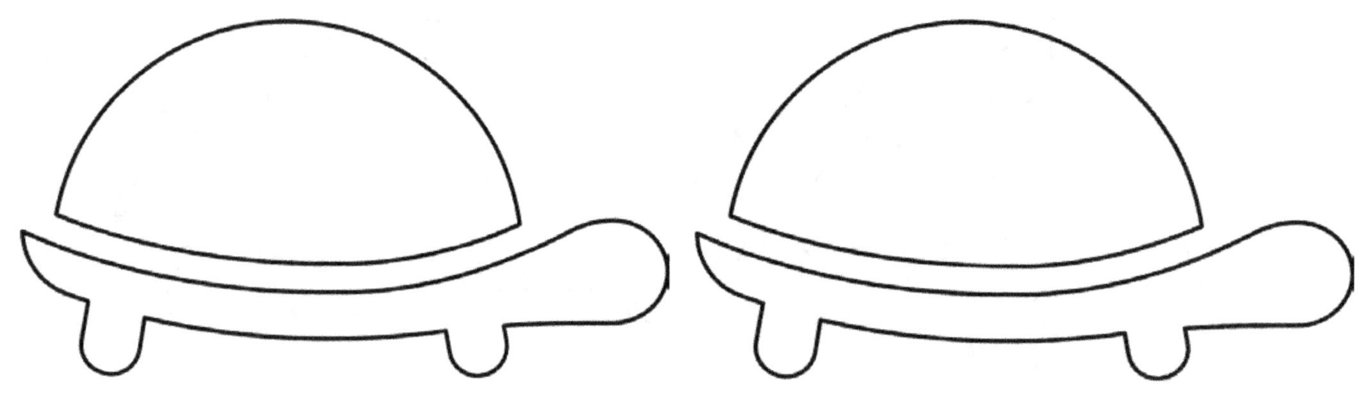

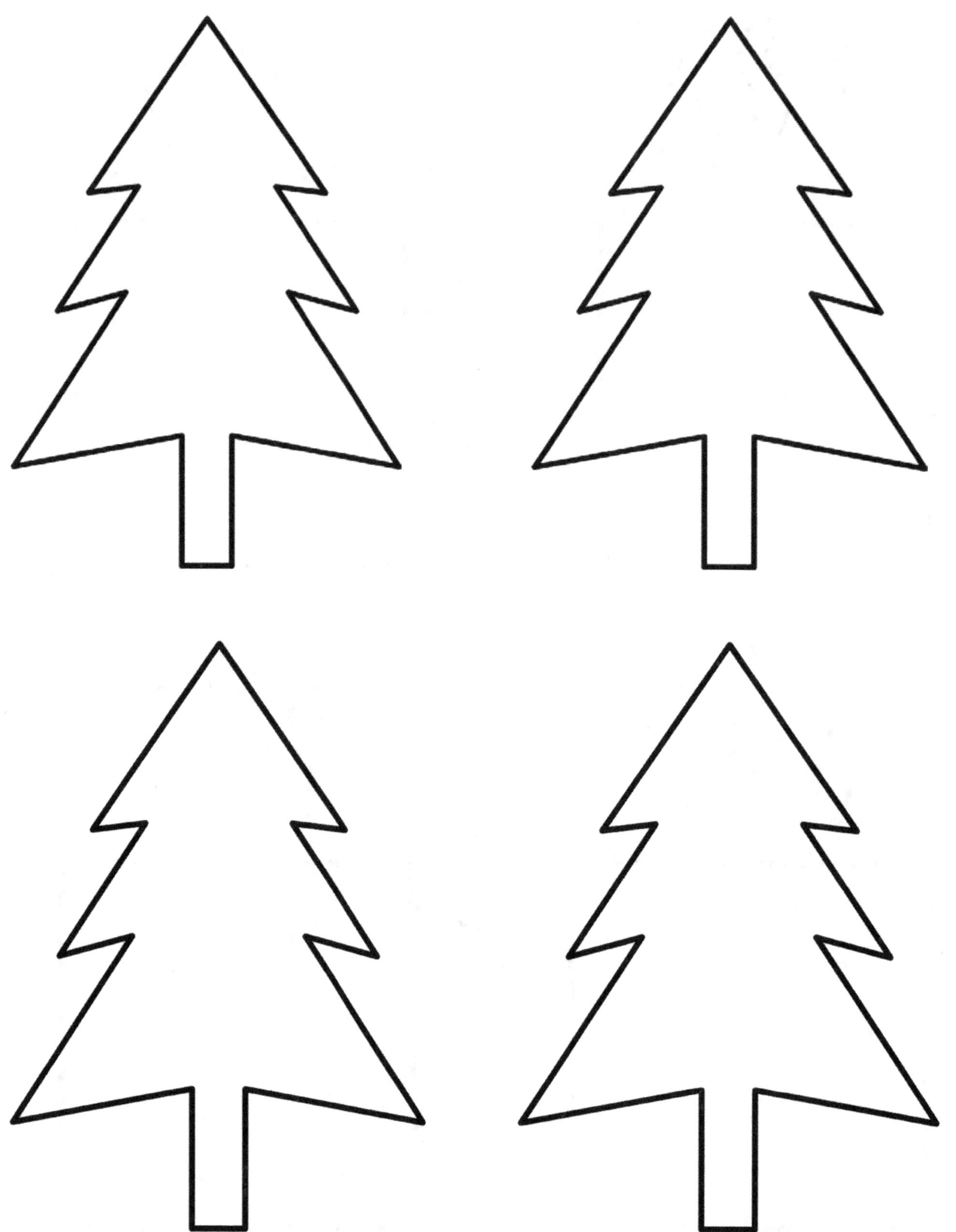

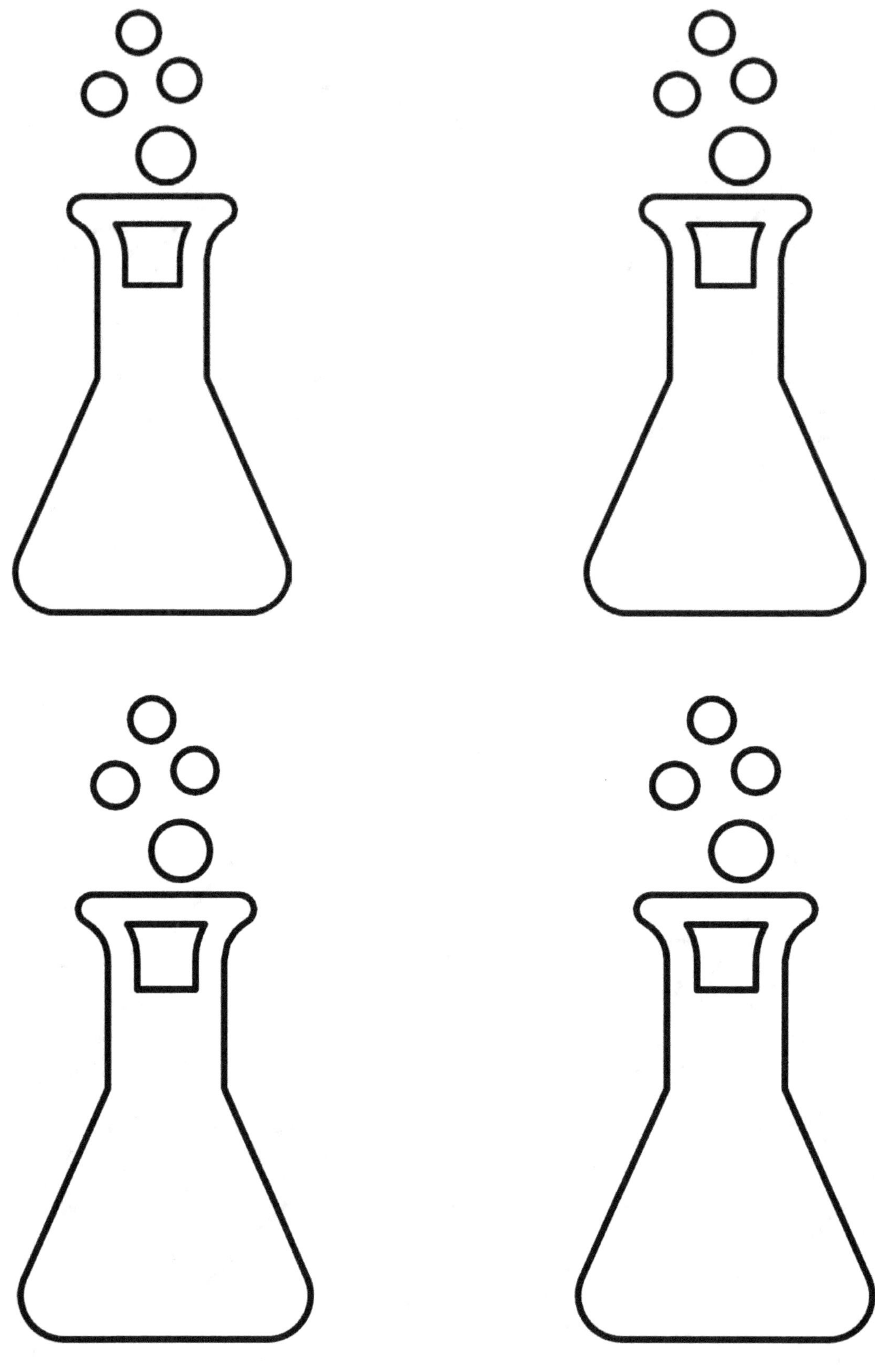

END